MW01688330

Network Marketing Secrets

Russell Brunson

Legal Disclaimer And Terms Of Use

This book is for research purposes only. All of the webpages and advertising is copyrighted by the original owners. You may borrow the 'ideas' in these ads and pages, but you may NOT use any of the actual advertising copy or designs.

You do not have resell rights or giveaway rights to any portion of this Publication. Only customers that have purchased this publication are authorized to view it. This publication contains material protected under International and Federal Copyright Laws and Treaties. No part of this publication may be transmitted or reproduced in any way without the prior written permission of the author. Violations of this copyright will be enforced to the full extent of the law.

The information services and resources provided in this book are based upon the current internet marketing environment. The techniques presented have been extraordinarily lucrative and rewarding. Because the internet is constantly changing, the sites and services presented in this book may change, cease or expand with time. We hope that the skills and knowledge acquired from this course will provide you with the ability to adapt to inevitable internet evolution. However, we cannot be held responsible for changes that may affect the applicability of these techniques.

Any earnings, income statements or other results, are based on our own testing and are only estimates of what we think you could earn. There is no assurance you will do as well as stated in any examples. If you rely upon any figures provided, you must accept the entire risk of not doing as well as the information provided.

Screenshots in this book are from publicly accessible field archives. All product names, logos and artwork are copyrights of their respective owners. None of the owners have sponsored or endorsed this publication. While all attempts have been made to verify information provided, the author assumes no responsibility for errors, omissions, or contrary interpretation on the subject matter herein. Any perceived slights of peoples or organizations are unintentional. The purchaser or reader of this publication assumes responsibility for the use of these materials and information. No guarantees of income are made. The author reserves the right to make changes and assumes no responsibility or liability whatsoever on behalf of any purchaser or reader of these materials.

TABLE OF CONTENTS

INTRODUCTION

I ran home from school, bursting through the door. I was 13 or 14 years old at the time, and saw the package sitting there on the kitchen counter. I can still remember the butterflies in my stomach when I saw that cassette tape sitting on top of a pile of junk mail. I grabbed it, ran to my room, and tore it open.

A combination of fear and excitement and nervousness set in. It's the same feeling you get at the top of a roller coaster when you peek over the edge just before a giant drop. It was exhilarating and frightening all at the same time.

Unlike most teens, I had this strange habit of collecting junk mail for business opportunities. It started after I found a magazine and called every 1-800 number I could find. I wanted their "free information." Within weeks, I was getting 10 to 20 letters a day from people offering me the latest get-rich-quick schemes. It was awesome.

But this cassette tape was different. It wasn't like the others. It was special. I plugged the tape into my Walkman and started listening. The voice on the other end was a man talking about a product that he knew would change the world. He spoke with so much passion and conviction, it made me believe every word he said.

After talking about the product for almost an hour, he mentioned a new opportunity. He explained how it worked, and how I could make money by sharing this message with others. Unfortunately for me, as a 14 year old, I didn't have a credit card, and I couldn't convince my parents to listen to the tape. And so my first journey into network marketing ended before it even started.

But still, I remember that feeling.

Over the next 23 years of my life, I had all sorts of network marketing experiences. I built companies as a distributor, I was a top money earner, and I cofounded a highly successful network marketing company.

I've watched as companies have come and gone.

I've seen new entrepreneurs get started and succeed at mind-boggling levels while others go out of business without making a dime.

I've also watched people who were extremely successful at growing their companies offline fail horribly when they tried to make the transition into the online world.

As one of the founders of the software company ***ClickFunnels***, the #1 question I get almost every day is...

“Can I use sales funnels to grow my network marketing company?”

I always smile at this question, because 99% of ***ALL*** network marketing companies were built using the ***SAME THREE FUNNELS*** (offline).

Yet for some crazy reason, when people start doing business online, they completely forget how these three funnels have worked for them and all the leaders in their companies.

Instead, they jump online and try out whatever fad is new and exciting at the time, and completely forget the ***CORE STRATEGY***, the core ***FUNNELS*** that have brought them success up to that point.

This article will take you behind the scenes of the three funnels that have built 99% of ALL successful network marketing companies, and show you how to replicate them online with simple sales funnels. You'll be able to plug your network marketing opportunity into these funnels within just a few minutes.

I'll also tell you the **one step that everyone forgets**. Miss this step and your funnels will never gain the momentum you need to be a top earner.

Ready? Good. Me too!

Section #1

THE THREE LOST FUNNELS

Secret One: The Evolution of the Network Marketing Funnel

Before I explain the three lost funnels and how they work, I first want to walk you through the journey that most new distributors go through when they join any new network marketing opportunity. My guess is that as you read through these steps, you'll probably identify phases you've already been in, or ones you are in now.

It's interesting, because almost everyone who has asked me, "Can I use sales funnels to grow my network marketing company?" is stuck in one of these phases, yet those who use the three funnels (both offline and online) actually bypass all of them.

The goal *ISN'T* to get through the phases, it's to step **outside the phases** and build your empire on a completely different foundation (which I'll show you in the next chapter).

So sit back, relax, grab some popcorn, and let's go on this quick journey together.

Phase #1: The NFL Club

After joining your first network marketing company, the first thing you are told is to talk to your friends and family about the products and the opportunity you have. The problem is that if your family members—the people you respect the most—don't sign up, or if they talk negatively about the opportunity you're offering them, it can be devastating. In fact, a huge percentage of people drop out almost immediately after talking to loved ones first.

Even if you make it past this first round and your family supports you, eventually the exhaustion factor kicks in. You run out of people and friends to sell to. And if you try to sell to the same group of people again and again, they get exhausted by you and your message. Eventually, they avoid you completely. When this happens, you get inducted into a group we like to call the NFL (No Friends Left) Club.

Social media has made our networks a bit larger, but it's still a finite pool of people. After posting a few selfies with your new product or asking them to message you if they are ready to quit their jobs or lose weight, you'll quickly find that you're fishing in a pond that usually isn't too interested in what you're selling.

And that is why growing through friends and family is so hard. Because instead of going ***OUTSIDE*** their network to scale, a lot of people just beat down the same doors again and again as they watch their response rates get lower and lower with each post. And well... it's because they don't know what else to do.

Phase #2: The Anti-Sales Department

The second phase usually starts as soon as the first phase is ending. With the few interested family and friend responses you have, when they are ready to buy, you send them to what we call the "anti-sales department," or your company's corporate website. Most of the websites look beautiful, but they are not set up to get people to actually buy something. They are bad at converting your visitors into customers. Scratch that... **they just suck.**

Most good network marketers can sell any product really well. Even if you can get your mom or your aunt or uncle to fall in love with the product, and even if you've set up the sale perfectly, you have to send them to the company to actually buy, and the shopping cart often confuses them with a horrible and outdated buying experience.

The site may have too many options, an outdated shopping cart, and no understanding of cart value or conversion rates. These company websites aren't able to keep the emotional connection to the buyer that you started. And on and on it continues.

Imagine you're out at a party and there's a woman you ***REALLY*** want to ask out to dinner. You go up to her and you're so smooth and it's awesome and you're ready to take down her number. But right at that moment, you have to stop and say,

"Okay, before I take down your number, I'm going to hand you off to my Grandpa, who doesn't know how to use a cell phone, loves to tell you all kinds of stories with completely unimportant details, and has really bad breath. But it's okay. He'll get your information."

Even if she wanted to go out with you, she probably won't because you handed her off to Grandpa.

Buzzkill. Lost date. Better luck next time.

That's what it's like to send interested buyers to corporate company websites. These sites are built by lawyers, not marketers, so they do the ***OPPOSITE*** of what you want. They actually repel people and push them away instead of hooking them in.

Phase #3: The Clone Wars

The third phase sneaks up on you, usually about the time you're ready to go outside your network and look for new people to sell to. You're squarely in the NFL Club, and you know that if you don't go after people outside your network, this opportunity will be over.

That's when you enter... ***The Clone Wars.***

At this stage, you're diving into internet marketing to find your leads, drive traffic, and make sales. But then... a realization.

Although your company's owners are bragging about their numbers, they are giving everyone in their 300,000+ member network marketing company the **exact** same template and products and instructions for how to sell.

They are creating ***MASSIVE*** competition for you.

Statistics show that 98% of businesses fail, and that's when they are selling unique products and in a space without thousands of identical competitors. Imagine the statistics if everyone were selling the same thing in the same way as a million other people.

When 300,000 team members using the ***SAME*** template with ***NO*** variation whatsoever, and those 300,000 people all try to run the same ad and social media campaigns, what happens? People get used to it and start to tune you out. Instead of it grabbing people's attention, it just becomes an expected pattern to ignore.

In order to succeed online, you need to always keep the concept of **Pattern Interrupt** in your mind. This means doing things differently, keeping your audience excited, building and customizing your own funnels that interrupt their daily patterns.

People who escape Phase #3 realize that funnels and internet marketing strategies are so important, and implementing the company's massive cookie-cutter plan is not that effective.

Phase #4: The Homeless Man With a Ferrari

Not everyone gets to the fourth phase. In fact, most network marketers can't get out of the earlier phases to even experience this one. So I'll tell you what happens.

Phase #4 is when you make enough money selling the product that you start to think this actually might be a profitable venture. But then you're hit with the "homeless man with a Ferrari" problem.

After a bunch of failed tries in multilevel marketing, I took another opportunity and used everything I was learning about funnels and internet marketing, and it seemed I had finally cracked

the code. Within just 90 days, I had sold enough product to win a Ferrari through the network marketing company I was promoting!

There was just one problem. Within a year, my commission checks had gone down to almost zero. Can you believe it? I had become the homeless man, with no money but a really sweet car.

Okay, okay, I wasn't actually homeless. But if this had been my only stream of income, I would have been! Why had this happened?

I failed to understand one of the core foundations to network marketing: **Duplication.** My leads didn't know how to create and sell to their own leads as well.

I had won a sales contest and a car, but hadn't built any long-term plan for residual income with a downline.

I began to really study this concept, along with funnels, because I could tell these two parts were the key to it all.

Escape the Phases With Funnels!

Going back to the roots of how network marketers grow, there is a reason some people are ***SO*** successful at network marketing and bypassing all these phases I just talked about.

They aren't selling to friends and family every day. They aren't spamming social media. They don't rely on cookie-cutter cloned templates and the anti-sales department to finish the sale. They don't forget about the important of Duplication and residual income through a downline.

The ones who are growing use three core funnels, and that's what we're going to talk about next.

Secret Two: The Three Lost Funnels

Funnels are not hard (don't let anyone tell you otherwise), and they are not magic. In fact, **all the top earners online were using funnels in their business...** in real life. They simply took what worked so well offline then replicated it online!

Funnels are not new, they are not magic, and we're not

reinventing the wheel.

We're not going to deviate from what already works and has been proven in the real world. We're simply taking the process and making an online version of it. You see so many people trying all these fancy tactics and spammy offers—this is not that.

The three funnels online repeat the same proven concepts that have worked in network marketing for decades.

The online funnels mimic the effectiveness of real-life selling. They create an automated system where we can get leads to come to us, we can sell to them, and most importantly, we can Duplicate!

In order to build these funnels quickly, let's identify the selling process that happens in real life so you can see how to make it work inside a funnel.

Lost Funnel #1: The Bridge (aka Three-Way Calls)

When you study those who have built great teams, you see they understand that when they first bring someone onto their team, that is when they are most vulnerable. They know the least about the product and they have fears about the prospects they are going to present the opportunity to, because they don't have any credibility or their own story yet.

So what they will often do is have the upline get on a three-way call with you, their newest team member, and your potential customer. The upline leader will then take the stress and fear away from you, and discuss the product and opportunity with your friend. You introduce the leader, and they tell the story and then ask for the sale.

They create a "bridge" between you and the product / opportunity you are offering your friend.

After you work with your upline leader a few times, you are able to see the process, have your own experiences with the product, and feel more comfortable telling your stories about why you believe in the product / company. At this point, you can create your own bridge between your prospect and the product / opportunity you are offering them.

Those who grow big teams understand that, by having someone else help them to create the bridge initially, the new network marketer can learn the ropes and feel comfortable with selling, before they have a lot of experience. They get on three-way calls with their new members, help them to close sales, and guide them to understand the process.

That is how Duplication happens offline by using three-way calls. It works today, it worked yesterday, and it will continue to work forever.

When we come online, this process does not change. For some reason, when people come online, they go crazy trying the exciting new shiny way to get leads, but if you want those leads to sign up ***AND*** be able to get others to sign up, you need to follow the fundamentals.

As you will see in Section Three, we replicate this same process online with a funnel we call the **Bridge Funnel.**

Lost Funnel #2: Home Party Selling

I still remember the first time my wife told me she was going to an essential oils home party. As a marketing guy, I was so excited, I begged her to take me along.

She was so embarrassed that I wanted to go with her, but I wanted to see the home party in action and see what I could learn from the process. So we got a babysitter for the kids, and off we went.

I was the only guy in the room, so I kind of hid in the back and kept quiet so I wouldn't raise any extra attention that would embarrass my wife.

I carefully watched how the demo unfolded and how the party host transitioned to the sales pitch. There was a powerful atmosphere in the room because the guests were watching the demos, hanging out with other people who were interested. You could feel the excitement growing.

This particular host was really nervous and didn't even sell all that well, and even though the pitch wasn't perfect, the host telling her stories about the essential oils and demonstrating the products— these actions did most of the selling already.

Home parties work because people are able to experience the product in a nonpressurized sale setting. There's also the added benefit of ***"FOMO"***—the fear of missing out. When people see others buying, it helps them to buy more as well.

Now the power behind home parties isn't just the products that are sold there. The real power comes when the host explains how she got a bunch of free products for hosting the party and asks if anyone else would like to host one! They can either do it as a favor for free products, or they can join the opportunity by hosting themselves, and the host would help them run their first party.

This is how one party turns into four or five other ones. This is how Duplication happens with home parties.

Once again, for some reason when people go online, they forget the tried and true principles they've used to grow their company offline. In fact, the first time I ever saw true Duplication online was when I created a Home Party Funnel. (I'll explain how it works in Section Three, but I want to share the results we got from it here.)

I used the Home Party Funnel to help generate over 1.5 million leads in a new company in just six weeks...and grew my own personal leg to the third largest in the company during that time!

Unlike real-life home parties, the Home Party Funnel can actually **keep** the party going, even after the live event ends. We'll dig more into this in a bit.

Lost Funnel #3: The Hotel Meeting

The very first hotel meeting I went to, I was invited by a friend. My friend basically said to me, "Hey, I went to this meeting the other day. This guy is making crazy money, and he's doing another presentation tomorrow. Do you want to come?"

I don't know about you, but for me, the answer to that question is always ***YES!***

When I arrived, there were about 40–50 people in the room. My friend told me that the previous week there had only been about 10 people, but since each person had brought a few friends, the group was growing quickly.

Sure enough, the presenter did a great job on stage. He sold the product and he sold the opportunity. But then he did something special, which was the reason he ended up building the largest team inside his company, eventually making millions.

He told those who signed up at the end of the presentation that he was going to be back the following week giving this same presentation, and if they wanted him to close their friends for them, they needed to bring them to that meeting.

So simple, so powerful. That last step is how he created the Duplication that grew his team.

The next week, there were 75 people in the room. Then 150. Within a very short time period, he was hosting weekly meetings with 400–500 people.

The Hotel Meeting Funnel is designed to...

- **Introduce prospects to the product**
- **Create the opportunity to make money**

- **Show how they can grow their own teams by bringing people to the meetings**

This triple punch is powerful because the presentation is usually done by someone who has experienced some level of success in the company, you can relate to the story, and you want it to be your story, too.

This type of selling is designed to recruit ***NEW LEADERS***, not just product lovers.

When we pull this model onto the internet and into funnel world, we call this the **Hotel Meeting Funnel.**

Who are you talking to?

With each of these scenarios, you're talking to someone—a person who may be interested in the product or who's interested in the business opportunity. How do you figure out who to talk to and in what funnel?

People ask me all the time, "Do I make a funnel to sell more stuff, or to fill my downline, or what?"

You can do both.

Here's what I discovered works best...

Secret Three: Your Two Dream Clients

Unlike most businesses who sell to one specific type of customer, when you join a network marketing opportunity, you actually have ***TWO.***

Yes, you have two completely different types of customers. This doesn't mean they can't be the same person, or start as one type and become the second type. But here's a quick picture of your two dream client types. (And in a minute, I'll explain why understanding this is so important to not messing up your funnel.)

The "I Love This Product" People vs. The "I Love Selling Stuff" People

Suzy + John

The "I love this product" people are all about the product.

They come to the party. They see the product. They get excited. They want to lose more weight or have more energy, and get so excited about the product. They want the results and transformation the product brings to their lives.

Karen + Steve

The "I love selling stuff" people are the business builder types who want to sell.

These people don't really care as much about the product. They just love to sell stuff. They want to make sure the product is good, but it's more important that the product sells well because they just want to sell, sell, sell.

In marketing, we call this an ideal customer **avatar.** Two different customers with two different motivations. Suzy and

John are motivated by the results the products give. They don't really want to be entrepreneurs. Karen and Steve on the other hand are probably not as interested in the product results, but will jump at the chance to make more money!

I know what you're thinking:

"Well, I actually know people like Suzy and John, and they buy the product and love it so much, they start telling friends about it, and then ***THEY*** start selling it!"

I know! It's awesome, right? And this is really possible, too. You can absolutely leverage this reality, but you have to do it strategically.

What to Lead With in Your Funnel

When you create one of the three lost funnels—a Bridge Funnel, a Home Party Funnel, or a Hotel Meeting Funnel—you must always be speaking to just ONE of your dream clients, not both at the same time.

We can't confuse TWO sales messages in our campaigns because they get diluted. We can hint at it (and I'll show you how), but a confused buyer doesn't buy.

Your funnel either needs to lead with the product, and then during your presentation you introduce the opportunity (use this model if you are more like Suzy and John above), or your funnel leads with the opportunity, and then during your presentation you introduce the products (use this model if you are more like

Karen and Steve).

This way, you ascend someone from the product to the opportunity, or from the opportunity to the product.

The real power of the internet comes when you build a funnel to attract each of your dream clients. You have one funnel to bring in people who will become passionate about the product, and then you have another one to bring in builders and leaders to grow your team.

But to begin with, just create one. Master one, learn how to drive traffic to one.

The THING You Must Master For Effective Online Funnels

Now that you can see the three core real-life selling scenarios that match up to the lost funnels, we're going to dig in and go step-by-step to show you how to build them online...within minutes.

But here's a warning: There is ***ONE*** thing you must master in order to ensure that every funnel you set up is profitable. It doesn't matter which funnel you choose first, but all three of them must have this dialed in, or this system doesn't work.

This is where most people mess up. They follow up to this point, they understand the real-life selling and how it should be replicated online, but then they fail to complete this next part. So don't skip it!

It's called the **Viral Loop.**

The Viral Loop is a selling sequence that occurs in each of the three lost funnels, and guarantees you're hitting all the points you need to hit in order to make a sale. The Viral Loop has four key components:

- **Epiphany Bridge**
- **Demo**
- **Call to Action**
- **Duplication**

Let's examine each of these in detail...

Section #2

THE VIRAL LOOP

Secret #4: The Epiphany Bridge: How to Sell Without Selling

The Viral Loop is the key to not only selling someone on your network marketing opportunity, but also to getting those you recruit to create Duplication that will grow your downline.

Inside this section, we will walk through the four phases of the Viral Loop. The first phase is a concept we call the Epiphany Bridge Script.

The first time I shared this concept with anyone, I was speaking to the top leadership team at an annual event for a well-known network marketing company.

But before I went in to the event, I stood in the lobby watching some of the distributors who were waiting for the meeting to start. They were trying to prospect people in the lobby. You could tell they were die-hard fans of their respective network marketing companies, because they were covered in swag and carrying samples of their products, and had their sales pitches memorized.

I watched them try to talk to these new people, and many of them were committing the #1 sin of selling...without even realizing it. The victims...er...prospects looked scared and unsure, and some of them were even running away!

So what were these distributors doing?

They were logically trying to convince these prospects that their network marketing opportunity was the best. They shared the science behind why their products were better than their competitors. They talked about the research, the science, the ingredients, and more.

Although they thought they were selling, all they were really doing was spewing onto unsuspecting prospects what we call "technobabble."

My good friend Kim Klaver wrote a book called ***If My Product's So Great, How Come I Can't Sell It?*** She has a chapter in there all about technobabble and how it is the #1 killer of sales for network marketers.

As I walked into the room, ready to give my presentation, I stopped and looked out over the crowd. In this room were the top 120 distributors, the top network marketers in the company. Yet many of them were the same people I had seen in the lobby spewing out technobabble.

I knew they needed something completely different from what I had prepared. They needed to understand that people do not buy based on logic. They buy based on emotion. And to get that emotion, they needed to understand a concept I call the Epiphany Bridge.

I asked the group, "Why did you join this network marketing opportunity?"

Hands instantly shot up.

Some told me about the science, others said they joined because of the new technology that had created their products.

After listening to them for a few minutes, I stopped them, and told them they had all lied to me. As they sat, shocked and silenced, I then explained that none of them had joined this opportunity for any of those reasons.

However, each of them had a story, something that had caused them to join their company. They'd had an emotional experience. Then after they had that emotional experience, after they were emotionally sold, then they had started to geek out on their product. They studied the science behind it, they found out why their ingredients were better, and they tried to figure out how to logically justify their sales.

And then, the worst thing happened. They took all of that logic (which had NOT convinced them to join this network marketing opportunity) and used it to try to convince other people to join them.

People do not buy things based on logic; they buy based on emotion, then try to justify their purchase logically. If you then take that logic and try to use it as your sales tool, you will struggle as a network marketer.

When you tell your story about how you emotionally fell in love with the product or the opportunity, they will connect with that, and then they will logically convince themselves later. But the key is explaining your epiphany about why you fell in love with the product.

I then asked the distributors about the real reasons they had joined this network marketing opportunity. One by one, they

started telling these incredible stories. Stories with emotion, meaning, and aha moments. I drew a little picture of the Epiphany Bridge on the whiteboard, and I started to explain what this script is and why it's so effective.

The Epiphany Bridge Script

So many people ***FORGET*** what it felt like before they got ahold of the information that changed their lives. But you can't forget that, because it was that journey that led you to the product you're selling. The Epiphany Bridge Script helps your prospect go down that journey too so they can feel that moment of "Aha!"

This concept is ***SO*** important, I dedicated an ***ENTIRE*** chapter to it in my book, Expert Secrets. You can pick up a free copy of ***Expert Secrets here***.

The key to your sales success isn't about becoming an amazing salesperson, it's about telling your story in a way so people have the same epiphany you had. When they do have that same epiphany you had, they will sign up, just like you did.

Some people struggle at telling stories, so inside Expert Secrets, I actually show you the script we use to tell our Epiphany Bridge stories. I go into a lot more detail in the book, but I wanted to give it to you now, so you have it as a tool to use every day.

This is what the script looks like:

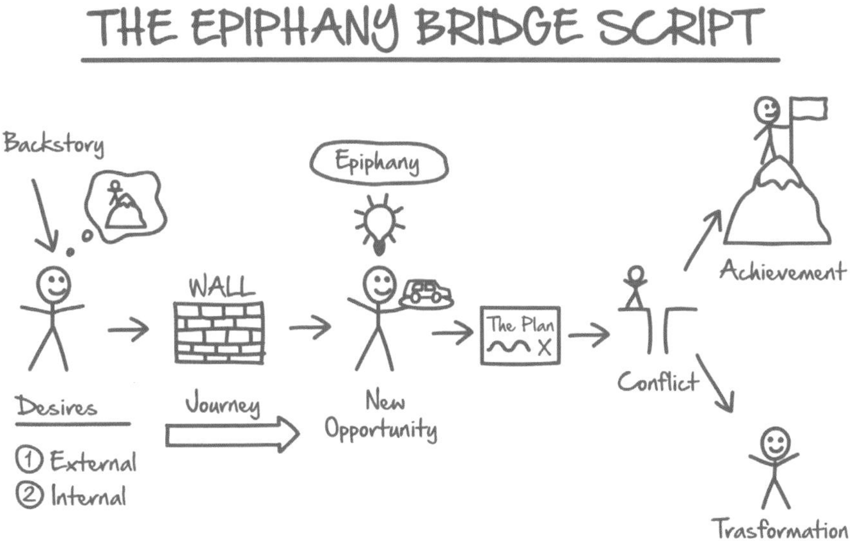

To walk you through the steps of this script, all you need to do is answer the questions below, and you'll tell your story in the correct sequence. To practice, have someone ask you the questions, then you give them the answers. Eventually you can take away the questions and just tell the answers, and this will create the perfect Epiphany Bridge Story.

Here are the questions:

- **Backstory:** What is your backstory that gives us a vested interest in your journey?
- **Desire:** What did you want to accomplish?
- **External:** What external struggle were you dealing with?
- **Internal:** What internal struggle were you dealing with?

- **Wall:** What wall or problem did you hit within your current opportunity to start you on this new journey?
- **Epiphany:** What was the epiphany you experienced and the new opportunity you discovered?
- **Plan:** What plan did you create to achieve your desire?
- **Conflict:** What conflict did you experience along the way?
- **Achievement:** What was the end result you achieved?
- **Transformation:** What transformation did you experience?

It sounds complicated, but it's really not. Again, if you want to learn about this in more detail, please get a free copy of my book ***Expert Secrets here***. And you can use it for little or big epiphanies. In fact, inside this report, I've told you multiple Epiphany Bridge stories already!

You'll be using the Epiphany Bridge Script to explain to people why you are involved in your network marketing opportunity in **every single funnel** and marketing effort you put out, that's just how important it is. It's the easiest way to sell without actually selling. It's the first step in the Viral Loop.

Secret Five: The Demo

The second step of the Viral Loop is the **demo.**

In this stage, you're showing the prospect the product you sell inside your network marketing company. If a picture is worth 1,000 words, a live demo is worth 10,000 or more! There's nothing quite like seeing and experiencing the product, and being able to ask questions of the seller.

In traditional offline marketing, you can let them sample the product, feel it, use it. Online it's harder, but you still need to do a demo of the product. The goal of the demo is to crush any objections the customer may have after hearing your Epiphany Bridge Story.

I learned what to say during a product demo from Billy Mays, one of the great infomercial kings of our time. He made hundreds of brands famous. I watched his commercials over and over to learn from him, and noticed some patterns that are really important to follow during the demo.

Here are a few of the powerful things you should include in your product demo.

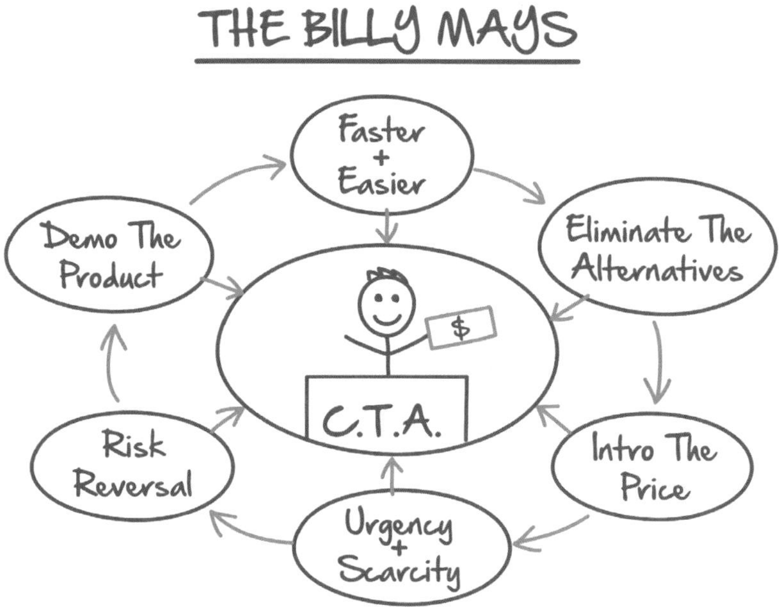

After introducing the product, the first thing you should do during a demo is something I call **Faster and Easier**. You'll want to find competing products or alternatives to what you're selling, and show how ***YOUR*** product is the faster or the easier choice.

Next, you want to make sure that during the Faster and Easier discussion, you've eliminated all the alternatives as options. If you haven't, try to figure out the unique selling point of your product that makes none of the competing products look appealing anymore. I call this **Eliminating Alternatives** in the demo.

Remember, you can just talk about this as you're demo-ing the product (making the shake, using the oil, cutting food with the knife, etc.).

Next, at some point in the demo, you want to **Introduce the Price** of the product. For example, if your oils are $25 a bottle, you could say something like:

"So these oils are $25 a bottle, but remember that one visit to the doctor and pharmacist can cost you $500 or more! With that kind of money, you could get 20 bottles and they would last you 5 years...for just the cost of one doctor's visit."

When your pricing is introduced, find something to compare or anchor it to.

Next, work in **Urgency and Scarcity**. Do you have any limited inventory or limited offers? If you're doing a party or a meeting, you can end the offer at the close of the meeting. Give people a reason to act ***NOW*** rather than later.

Then it's time for **Risk Reversal.** Explain your guarantee. Can they try it for 30 days and get a refund if they don't like it? I know people are scared of refunds, but they actually HELP people buy, because it takes the risk off of them and puts it on you. So during your demo, make sure to mention a guarantee that reverses the risk for the buyer.

There is one part we haven't discussed yet, the big circle in the middle: the Call to Action (CTA). That's the third critical piece of the Viral Loop, which we'll discuss next.

Secret Six: The Call to Action (CTA)

The **Call to Action** is the part that can make people nervous, but it is really easy when you do it right. It's where you ask for money in exchange for the product they are buying and close the sale. It's the step-by-step instructions that get interested buyers to the "finish line".

The funny thing is that the CTA for any network marketer is where most people get nervous. The first home party I attended, the woman who was selling did an ***AMAZING*** job with the demo, but when it came time for the pitch, she just froze. It was so awkward and uncomfortable. Don't do that!

One of the easiest ways to transition into a Call to Action is to transition by asking for permission. Yes, I actually ask them whether it's okay for me to sell them something. When they say yes (and they always do), all nerves and awkwardness instantly disappear.

"So you've heard and seen how this product has helped me (Epiphany Bridge), and I've just shown you here how it can help you (the demo), so I've put together a very special offer for you so you can have the same benefits I've had, and I'd like to go over them for a few minutes. Is that okay?"

When you tie back in your story and the demo and then ask a question, most people (if not all), will happily say yes (either out loud or in their heads). And they've just given you permission to give them an offer and a direct Call to Action.

The CTA should be clear and direct. Tell people what to do. Even things that seem completely obvious to you, say them anyway. You need to be ***VERY*** clear and direct about exactly what they need to do.

"To get this very special offer, contact the person who referred you to this webinar today. Tell them you want to get the ___________ offer, and they will get you signed up right away."

As you will see in Secret Seven, there will be others sending people into your funnels, so you can't just send them directly to your signup link, or you will lose out on the Duplication. You will be sending people back to talk to the person who referred them to see the demo.

The Call to Action should be given multiple times. As seen in the diagram above, you alternate between your demo script and a CTA. This way, they hear the instructions multiple times and in multiple different ways.

Secret Seven: The Ultimate Network Marketing Secret: Duplication

Lastly, we come to Duplication. Just a bit ago, I mentioned the importance of using the Epiphany Bridge stories to build trust, doing a product demo, and then giving them a clear CTA to close the sale. But there's one more step, and it's how to avoid becoming the homeless man with a Ferrari.

The key to making real money in your network marketing opportunity is **Duplication.**

Duplication happens when the people you get signed up for your network marketing opportunity start to refer others. This is the key to success.

The commissions for most network marketing companies on straight product sales isn't very high, so it's essential you help those who you recruit so they are able to recruit as well.

The reason I ***LOVE*** network marketing so much is because you aren't just paid by being the best at closing sales. You get paid by being the best at helping ***OTHERS*** to close sales. Developing others is how you get paid the big bucks. It's the most pure form of entrepreneurship I know of.

So how do you do that?

The key is understanding what people who mastered the three lost funnels offline do.

In the Bridge Funnel we shared in Secret Two, the person who recruits you doesn't just leave you alone. He or she then gets on the phone with you and does the next dozen sales with you, then trains you on how to do that with those you bring in!

In the Home Party Funnel, when the party's over, the host invites people to have parties at their homes, and she'll come and facilitate the party for you to teach you how to do it, so you can then start hosting parties for yourself (and for those who you recruit)!

In the Hotel Meeting Funnel, when the presentation is over, the presenter invites those who signed up to bring their friends to the following week's meeting so he can help get them signed up as well. The Hotel Meeting Funnel, we see this Duplication system working because the presenter does the work FOR the new distributors. All they have to do is bring some friends and their team builds effortlessly.

They've created a system for Duplication.

If we list it out as levels, it looks like this: **Level #1** is where you sign people up directly, **Level #2** is where you ask them to bring people into your funnel and you presell for them, and then **Level #3** is where you show them how to replicate what you've done with others.

When you are running any of the three funnels we'll be breaking down in the next section, the process to achieve Duplication is simple.

Level #1 > Sign the person up!

We've already gone through this in Secrets Four, Five, and Six. Use your Epiphany Bridge, Demo, and Call to Action to get them signed up for your product or opportunity.

Level #2 (first level of Duplication) > Have your people send others into your funnel.

If you are using the Bridge Funnel, after you sign up a new recruit, simply tell them, "Bring people into this funnel. It will convert them for you, and you'll get paid!"

If you are using the Home Party Funnel, after you sign up a new recruit, simply tell them,"Bring people into this funnel. It will convert them for you, and you'll get paid!"

If you are using the Hotel Meeting Funnel, after you sign up a new recruit, simply tell them, "Bring people into this funnel. It will convert them for you, and you'll get paid!"

Level #3 (second level of Duplication) > Share your funnel, and let them tell their own Epiphany Bridge Story.

After they have had success sending people into your funnels,

often times people will want to set up their own funnels and tell their own Epiphany Bridge stories.

Normally this process is pretty complicated, but if you are using ClickFunnels for your funnels, you can literally just send them what we call a "share funnel" link. When they click on that link, it will copy your funnel into their account! Then they can just go into the funnel and replace your videos with theirs. It's very simple.

In fact, at the end of this article, I will give you links for my three share funnels! You can click a button and within seconds you will be inside your ClickFunnels account. Then you just need to edit the pages and plug in your videos.

ClickFunnels makes all of this tons easier than any other tool, but more on that in a bit.

Okay, so now we're going to go into the mechanics of each

type of funnel and ***EXACTLY*** how to set it all up, but first make sure you've mastered the Viral Loop.

1. Use **Epiphany Bridge Scripts** to sell without actually selling.
2. Use the Billy Mays Script during your **Demo** to crush objections about the price and product.
3. Transition to a **Call to Action** with a question that gives you permission to sell.
4. Leverage the three levels of **Duplication** to find those first people on your team to do the job of building out your downline. Show them how to invite their friends so replication happens quickly and, when they are ready, let them tell their own Epiphany Bridge stories in their own funnels!

Section #3

DIGGING IN: THE THREE LOST FUNNELS

Secret Eight: Digging Into the Mechanics of the Three Lost Funnels

Okay, just to recap, here's where we're at.

- **In Secret #1**, we talked about the four phases of the average network marketer and why you must get OUT of that process and into a system that mimics what the top earners do instead.
- **In Secret #2**, we looked more closely at the three lost funnels and the selling scenario that happens in real life with each one that we will replicate online with our funnels.

- **In Secret #3**, we covered the two types of people who will come into your opportunity and how to position your funnel to attract each type.
- **In Secret #4**, we looked at the first step of the Viral Loop sequence, the Epiphany Bridge Script. We learned that we must KILL technobabble and use stories to help our prospects have aha moments that will inspire action.
- **In Secret #5**, we went to the second step of the Viral Loop, the demo. During the demo, it's important to crush objections while showing the product at the same time.
- **In Secret #6**, we transitioned to the third step of the Viral Loop, the Call to Action. This is where you take the prospect's hand, tell them exactly what to do, and walk them step-by-step through the checkout process.
- **In Secret #7**, we looked at the last step of the Viral Loop, the power of Duplication. Duplication is getting those you bring into your network marketing opportunity to pull others into those same funnels as well.

The next three secrets will focus on the mechanics of the three lost funnels, how to build them, and plug ***ANY*** opportunity into them within just a few minutes.

One last thing—I want to make sure we're on the same page about what a sales funnel actually is.

What is a sales funnel, really?

It's not cake or a kitchen tool. It's a term online marketers use to describe a series of web pages and emails. Yep, that's it—**web pages and emails.** What makes a funnel different from a website is that the emails and web pages are ordered in such a way that they create a path for your customer so they are more likely to do ***WHAT YOU WANT***. So rather than building a website where you land on a page and have 8,500,000 choices, a funnel orders the pages in steps.

Step One > Go here and click this.

Step Two > Go here and click this.

Step Three > Go here and buy this.

The emails in a sales funnel are messages sent to keep people on track, because guess what—even when you give people step-by-step instructions, some will still veer off course and need to be reminded and encouraged to get back on the path. That's what the emails do!

Now if sales funnels are simply a series of interconnected web pages and emails, what about all that talk you hear about webinars and one time offers (OTO's) and squeeze pages and carts? They are just fancy names for the ***TYPE*** of webpage it is.

It's like knives. You have the chef's knife, bread knife, steak knife, etc. They are all sharp objects that could get the job done right? But we label them to describe what they are best used for.

It's the same with a funnel.

- **The squeeze page** is where you ***SQUEEZE*** out an email address from someone by using curiosity.

- **An OTO page** is a one-time-only offer you show your customer after they've purchased something.
- **A webinar page** either shows a live or prerecorded class that builds trust and sells your product.

In the next few chapters, we're going to go into detail about how to easily create each of these funnels, without needing to know code, graphic design, or anything complicated.

We're going to do this with a tool called ClickFunnels, which achieves in 30 minutes what used to take me 3 months, a whole team, and thousands of dollars.

I remember when I would get a great idea for a new marketing campaign. I would get so excited and then, just as quickly, so depressed. Why? Because I knew it would take a huge team of people to pull it off. I'd need designers and coders and, like, three months.

Who has time for that? Not me!

That's why I created ClickFunnels. (More on that later.) We're going to tackle all of those problems in one fell swoop—easily and without a lot of pain, I promise.

Secret Nine: Digging Into The Bridge Funnel

Overview

The Bridge Funnel is a way for you to act **as the bridge** between the prospect and the company you represent. The Bridge Funnel mimics the three-way meeting and ensures that your prospect will walk through the process all the way to the sale, and not get lost or confused along the way.

The most important part of this entire funnel is you telling your Epiphany Bridge Story when you go through the Viral Loop. Be sure to review the Viral Loop so you make sure you cover all the important points. It's what really drives the emotion in the prospect and highlights the results they want to get from the product.

The only thing left to do in this funnel is to offer the product and walk them through how to actually get it. This way, they won't be confused by the checkout system or cart that the company uses.

So now that you know the purpose of the Bridge Funnel, it's time to build it!

The Step-by-Step Instructions

The Bridge Funnel has two pages you create, and then one page you direct them to (the company product page).

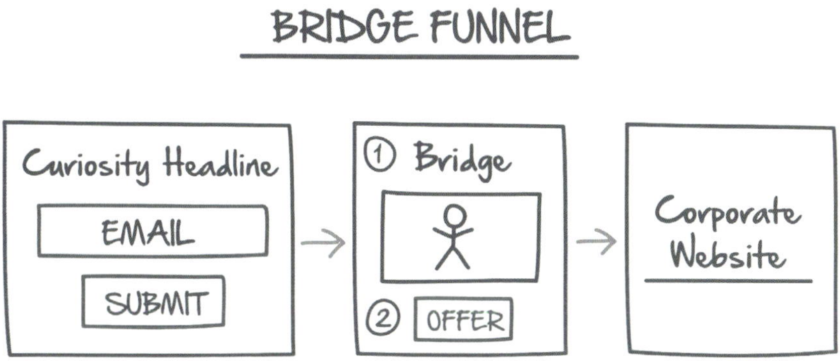

Page One: Hook 'em with curiosity.

The first page takes about three minutes to set up. (Or just one minute if you grab my free funnel template at the end of this article!) This page is all about curiosity. There are only two things you need to know about your prospect:

- **What they desire most**
- **What pain they want to avoid**

Then you simply create a headline using this format: "How to [what they desire most] without [the pain they want to avoid]."

In our example, the headline might read...

How to ace all your exams at school without losing focus or getting distracted during study time

Add that to the page along with a tagline that reads "This works even if you hate __________ [something else they may dread doing when trying to get the result they desire most]."

You're then going to create a form for them to input their email. From there, they will click a button to access page two of your funnel.

You might be wondering why this page is necessary. Remember the job of the emails in the funnel? Once you have their email address, you will be able to email them and help them ***REMEMBER*** you, your cool offers, and the way you can better their lives. Having their email gives you the ability to follow up. So think of Page One like the gatekeeper to your real offer.

Page Two: The Viral Loop Sequence Video with your Epiphany Bridge Story, Demo, and Call to Action

Page Two is simple to set up as well. It contains a video element and a button. That's it! Most of your effort here will be to create a powerful video script that covers everything outlined in the Viral Loop sequence.

Here's how it works, depending on the level of Duplication you're using.

Level #1: If you are the only person using this funnel, then the Call to Action (CTA) at the end of the video is to click on a button to go to the corporate website through your distributor link to sign up. I HIGHLY recommend in that video actually showing them the order form and how to fill it out so they don't get confused when they click and are taken to the corporate "anti-sales" department.

Level #2: If others are sending people into this funnel, you can't just link to the order form through your distributor link, because then you would be signing up their visitors. So instead the CTA in your video should tell them to get back in contact with the person who sent them into the funnel. That way they can follow up by sending them their distributor ID.

Level #3: The third option is to use a share funnel link for the funnel you've created, and allow others to copy your funnel into their accounts, keep your video (or create their own videos), and then change the link in the button to point to their own distributor links. That way, they get credit for each person they sign up.

Secret Ten: Digging Into the Home Party Funnel

Overview

The Home Party Funnel is one of my favorite funnels for network marketing. It does a lot of the same things as the Bridge Funnel, but with more fun and fanfare. We want to bring that party/hangout feel online and create a lot of sales within a short period of time. Not only that, we also want our parties to continue making sales after they have ended.

The actual funnel setup is only three pages. You'll set up an event invite page, then a thank-you confirmation page, and finally the hangout/party page.

So let's dive into the Home Party Funnel step-by-step.

The Step-by-Step Instructions

The Home Party Funnel has three pages, and then you send people to your company's sales page.

Page One: The Party Invite Page

The first page should have a great headline, tagline, picture, and description, as well as time, date, and input fields for your party. Make sure the button has a clear Call to Action like "Reserve my ticket to the __________ party."

Here are a few ways to create more bait on the page:

- **Add a timer.** This creates a sense of buzz and excitement.
- **Hint at a giveaway.** Perhaps everyone who attends live enters a drawing of some kind.

You'll do this party multiple times, so after the party ends, schedule the next one right on the same page, and just update the date and time.

Page Two: The Confirmation Ticket Page

Once they've registered, they will see a simple page with words like "You're registered" or "Invite a friend" and then have social media share buttons. If you run a Facebook group or Instagram account, you can encourage them to check you out over there between then and when the party begins.

Since you've collected their email address, it's good if you can write a few emails with reminders and the link to the party hangout page. People need regular reminders, so consider an email sequence that includes the following:

- **Confirmation Email**
- **Day-Before Email**
- **One-Hour-Before Email**
- **Party's Live Email**

Page Three: The Party Hangout Page

The party hangout page needs to have three main sections. The first section will have the headline, date, and time. The second section will have the live stream where you will be hosting the event. The third section will include images and buttons of the products you're featuring, with your distributor links to the company website where they can purchase the products and join the opportunity. You can also add a comment section where people can ask questions and give live feedback.

Now, imagine this hangout is just like a home party. You are going to be using all of the steps in the Viral Loop, but instead of just a video like you have in the Bridge Funnel, this is actually a ***LIVE*** event that people register for, and then have a chance to come and participate in! And as I'll show you below, if they miss the live stream, they can instantly see a recorded replay until the next live event starts! I'm going to take you through my tips for live streaming a party, and after a few tries, you'll be a pro, too.

How to Live Stream a Party

You'll need live-streaming software, but the easiest one to use is ***FREE***. It's called YouTube Live. Simply sign up for a YouTube account, then click on Events and Enable Live Streaming.

Once that's done, you'll go into YouTube and create an event. Just input the time and date, give it a title, and click Save. YouTube will give you a unique link. When you paste that link in the video element on the ClickFunnels page, it will automatically create a live stream. And if you're not live yet, it'll show a countdown timer.

Just like a live home party, you'll want to pick the products that are the most interesting, popular, and easy to demo. If you need some extra personality to keep your product demos interesting, you can invite friends or other team members onto the party live stream for fun banter and questions and answers. YouTube Live allows up to nine people in a hangout. Unlimited numbers of people can watch.

On the day of the party, you'll want to have a few things set up. First, your products. Whether it's your home office, kitchen, or living room, make sure you have decent lighting and space to demo the products.

Next, be sure to plug your computer directly into your router or modem, and shut down any nonessential programs. You'll want to sign in to YouTube Live about an hour before the event, and click on the ***START*** button. This will ***NOT*** start the event, but it will open up the software that allows you to broadcast.

Once inside the software, you can use tools like the Lower third to put your name and tagline, or even some of the fun hat and party effects. Click on the little person with the plus sign "To invite others..." into the party hangout room. You can have up to nine people on camera, and these people will be inside the hangout, not simply watching the live stream. It's good to get everyone inside within 15 minutes of starting so you can test microphones and cameras.

When it's time for the party to start, you'll hit the ***START BROADCAST*** button. At that point, you are live! That means everyone who has the party page link will be able to see you (and up to nine of your friends) live.

How to Keep the Party Going After it Ends

As you get used to these parties, you'll be able to do them weekly. Once your party is done, you can send a few follow-up emails to the registrants, so if they missed the live broadcast or want to watch it again, they can watch the replay. (YouTube Live just leaves the video up, so the party hangout page instantly becomes a replay page once it's done.)

Then simply switch out the date and time on the registration page to the next party. What happens is you have an ongoing stream of people watching the replay, a surge of people watching it live, and new registrants signing up each week. (We'll get to traffic after discussing the last of the three lost funnels.)

How to Make This Funnel Duplicate and Go Viral

While the Home Party Funnel works great for selling product, the real power comes when you get your team promoting it and you start getting true Duplication.

Level #1: If you are the only person using this funnel, then the (CTA) at the end of the home party is to click on the button to go to the corporate website through your distributor link to sign up. I ***HIGHLY*** recommend in that video actually showing them the order form and how to fill it out so they don't get confused when they click and are taken to the corporate "anti-sales" department.

Level #2: If others are sending people into this funnel, you can't just link to the order form through your distributor link, because then you would be signing up their visitors. So instead, the CTA in your home party should tell them to get back in contact with the person who sent them into the funnel. That way, they can follow up by sending them their distributor ID. You can link to your distributor's contact forms right underneath the live stream so it's one click to get in touch.

Level #3: The third option is to use a share funnel link for the product funnels you've created and allow others to copy your funnel into their accounts, keep your video (or create their own videos), and then change the link in the button to point to their own distributor links. That way, they get credit for each person they sign up. For the home party, you could give out share funnels for both products so they can recreate the home party for themselves.

Secret Eleven: Digging Into the Hotel Meeting Funnel

Overview

The Hotel Meeting Funnel is the last of our three funnels. It is actually my favorite of all funnels. I wish I could go into more detail here about all the ways you could write your script, structure your follow-up sequences and more, but it's outside the scope of this article.

However, I wrote an entire book teaching how to do webinar funnels, and you can get a free copy at ***www.ExpertSecrets.com***.

Before you geek out and try to optimize this funnel, I'll give you the blueprint you need to get one started fast.

As with the other two funnels, the actual funnel setup is three pages. You'll set up a registration page, then a countdown page, and finally, the webinar page. This funnel can be used live or prerecorded (so it works while you sleep).

So let's dive into the Hotel Meeting Funnel step-by-step.

The Step-by-Step Instructions

Page One: The Registration Page

The registration page is nearly ***IDENTICAL*** to the one for the Home Party Funnel. It includes a headline, tagline, input fields, time, and date. If you're running the Hotel Meeting Funnel on autopilot, it'll allow the viewer to choose a date to attend the virtual meeting, or they can choose to watch a replay—perfect for those who don't want to wait. If you're running it live, it will have the future date and time just like the Home Party Funnel.

Underneath the signup, you'll want to add three main bullets: the ***THREE SECRETS*** you're going to unpack in the workshop.

If you're not sure what kind of headline or secrets to use on the registration page, grab a copy of Expert Secrets, which details exactly how to write and script a webinar and registration page.

Page Two: The Countdown Page

This is, again, just like the Home Party Funnel thank-you page, but here we call it a countdown page.

Once they've registered, they will come to a simple page with words like "You're registered" or "Invite a friend" with social media share buttons. If you run a Facebook group or Instagram account, you can encourage them to check you out over there between then and when the party begins.

Since you've collected their email address, it's good to write a few emails with reminders and the link to the party hangout page. People need regular reminders so consider an email sequence that includes the following:

- **Confirmation Email**
- **Day-Before Email**
- **One-Hour-Before Email**

Page Three: The Webinar Page

The webinar page doesn't have much on it except the workshop title, the video element where your recording will go, and a button that leads to a form, email address, or other contact info. In ClickFunnels, you can create a delayed action so the button doesn't appear until the moment in your presentation when you announce it. The same goes for any free gifts you promise to those who stay until the end. These types of animations encourage people to watch and not click prematurely.

If you want people to be able to comment, you can also add a simple Facebook comments element under the video. Just be sure to check the comments each day to answer any questions.

The instructions above are for ***recorded webinars that autoplay.*** If you'd like to do the presentation live, you can either use YouTube Live like in the Home Party Funnel and just make it a more structured presentation, or you can use webinar software like Zoom or GoToWebinar, and eliminate the webinar page altogether.

As for what to say on the recording, refer to Section Two, the Viral Loop. Use the **Epiphany Bridge Script, Demo** the product so they can see how great it is to sell, and then the **Call to Action** needs to lead them to connect with you and become a part of the team.

How to Make This Funnel Duplicate and Go Viral

Level #1: If you are the only person using this funnel, then the (CTA) at the end of the Hotel Meeting Funnel is to click on the button below the video to sign up for the opportunity. I HIGHLY recommend in that video actually showing them how to fill it out so they don't get confused when they click and are taken to the corporate "anti-sales" department.

Level #2: If others are sending people into this funnel, you can't just link to your own contact form or distributor link, because then you would be signing up their visitors. So instead, the CTA should tell them to get back in contact with the person who sent them into the funnel. That way, they can follow up by sending them their distributor ID. You can link to your distributor's contact forms right underneath the live stream, so it's one click to get in touch.

Level #3: The third option is to use a share funnel link for the product funnels you've created, and allow others to copy your funnel into their accounts, keep your video (or create their own videos), and then change the link in the button to point to their own distributor links. That way, they get credit for each person they sign up. For the Hotel Meeting Funnel, you could give out share funnels for both products so they can recreate the hotel meeting for themselves.

Section #4

WHAT TO DO NEXT

Secret Twelve: How To Get Started RIGHT NOW!

I hope you're excited and ready to go blow up your business!

Here are the next steps:

We've created ***THREE*** **free premade and customized** share funnels that match the Bridge Funnel, Home Party Funnel, and the Hotel Meeting Funnel.

- **Download the Bridge Funnel Now!**
- **Download Your Free Home Party Funnel Now!**
- **Download Your Free Hotel Meeting Funnel Now!**
- **Share This With Your Network Marketing Friends**

You can download all three funnels at: https://networkmarketingsecrets.com/3secretfunnels

When you download the funnels, if you don't have a free trial of ClickFunnels yet, you'll be asked to set one up. As soon as you do, the funnel will be loaded into your account, and you can simply plug in your opportunity and get started!

After your funnel is live, you'll need to get some traffic into it. Traffic is a whole other topic, but Secret Thirteen has a few ideas to get you started.

You'll also be able to download this report in a PDF format so you can refer to it again and again.

Secret Thirteen: How To Fill Your Funnel

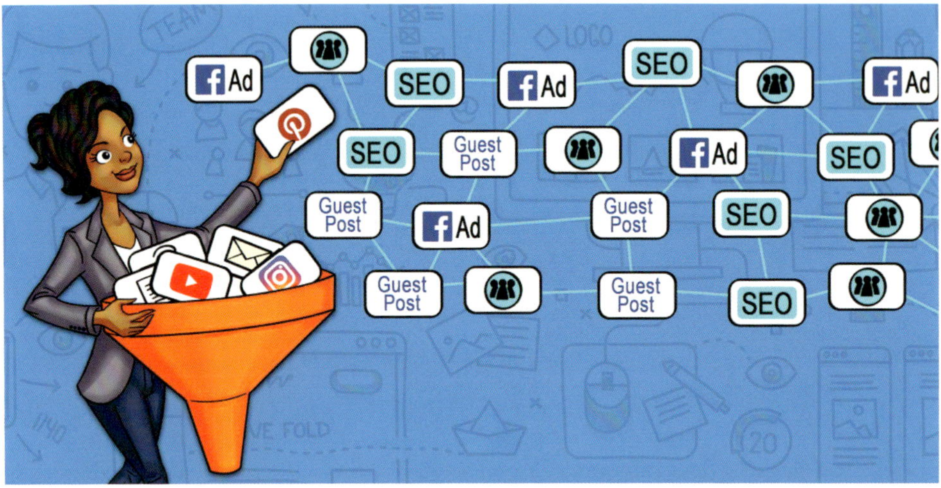

Once you've downloaded the funnels into your ClickFunnels account and have them set up, it's time to bring traffic to them. I wanted to briefly touch on the methods you can use to fill your funnels. Traffic is the fuel in your funnel. You'll need a steady stream of leads each day, opting in, so you always have a new supply of cash and possible team members. Here are some of the most popular ways to fill a funnel...

1. **Email Signature:** Place a link in your email signature inviting people to your Bridge or Home Party Funnel.

2. **Instagram Bio Link:** Place a link on your Instagram profile that gives something away for free.

3. **Your Own Facebook Group:** Build a free community around the topics that most interest your ideal customers.

4. **Facebook Ads:** This is one the most powerful ways to grow your business. Run ads to any of your funnels. (Just be careful about making business claims on your landing pages.)

5. **Other People's Groups:** Some groups allow for promotional posts and links. You can make great connections in big groups where your ideal customers hang out.

6. **Pinterest Pins to Blog Posts:** Set up a blog or a few signature pieces of content and make sure to include links to your free offers and funnels. Then pin beautiful images onto Pinterest that lead back to those blog posts.

7. **SEO (Search Engine Optimization):** Those same blog posts can also start to generate Google traffic if you do some keyword research on what people are searching for online.

8. **Guest Posting:** If the idea of writing your own blog feels overwhelming, you can reach out to other bloggers and offer to write a guest post. Most will allow you to put a link in your bio, and that can lead into your funnel.

9. **Podcasting:** Whether you decide to host your own podcast or just be featured on others, they are a great way to get the word out about your product.

10. **YouTube Channel:** For some companies, YouTube tutorials work really well. They are searchable with Google, and you can add annotated cards at the end of your videos that drive people to your offers and funnels.

There's actually a LOT more to traffic I'd love to share with you. In the next bonus chapter, I'll show you how to get free leads into your funnels!

If you're ready to share this book with your downline, you can get another copy of Network Marketing Secrets for your team at:

https://NetworkMarketingSecrets.com

I know there's been a lot of information in this article. Don't forget you can learn more about funnels inside my bestselling book, Expert Secrets at ExpertSecrets.com.

Remember, you're just one funnel away...

Russell Brunson

Bonus Chapter

FILL YOUR FUNNEL

Introduction: A Brief History Of Traffic

When I first started building sales funnels I had assumed that when the funnel was live, similar to the movie Field of Dreams that "If I built it, they would come..." but unfortunately I quickly found out that this was just not true.

After it was live, I waited for days, and no one showed up, ever. So, then I started looking for other ways that I could drive traffic. Back then there was a big online scam that I fell for, where you could pay someone a few thousand dollars, and they would submit your website to thousands of search engines. I assumed that was the secret, so I paid them a lot of money that I didn't have, and then waited for the people to start pouring into my funnels. But once again, nothing happened.

Then I started learning other tactics and techniques that people had that guaranteed I could get traffic, and while the people who were teaching them seemed like they meant well, when I tried to apply these strategies, I found that almost none of the techniques actually worked.

No matter what I tried, I had almost no luck. Looking back on it now, I realize that it's because I was trying different tactics, yet I didn't understand the overall strategy of how traffic works. As soon as I started to understand the strategies that I'm going to share with you in this booklet, I was able to get prospects and customers to start coming into my funnels with their credit cards in hand.

Inside of the DotCom Secrets and the Expert Secrets books, I don't get too deep into traffic, because the tactics behind how you get traffic on each platform (like Google, Youtube and Instagram) change often. Because of that, I didn't want to write something that would become obsolete the minute it was printed. I wanted to create something that would be evergreen so I didn't cover traffic much inside either of those books, and the same is true with this booklet. I want you to understand the strategies, but you will need to dig a little deeper into each platform to master the tactics on how they work. But after you understand the strategy, it's easy to outsource the tactics to others, or learn them yourself.

Now, to really understand how to get "traffic" or "people" into your funnels, it's helpful to go back and understand how people got traffic before the internet.

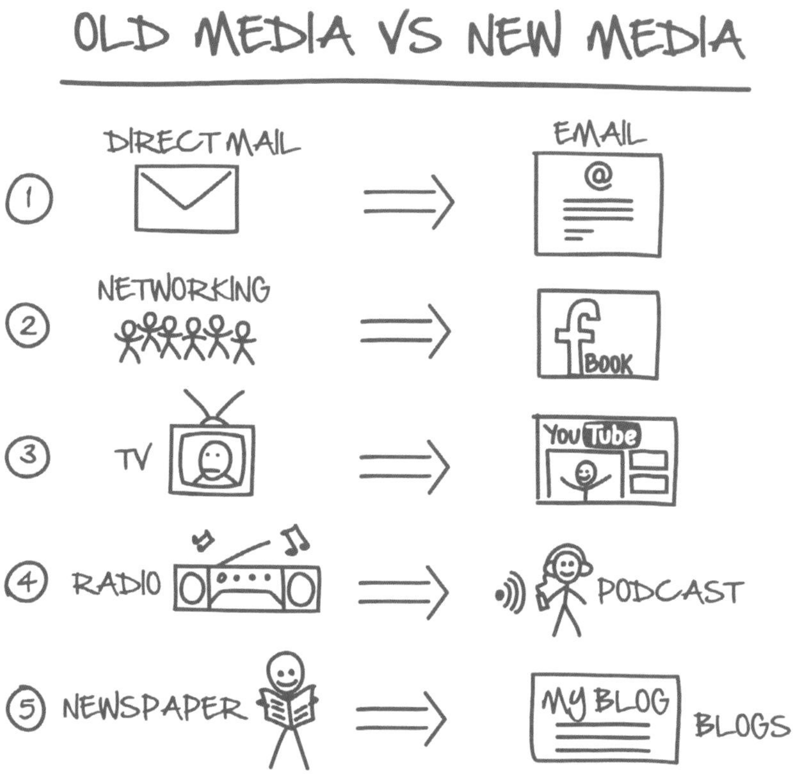

In the past, businesses didn't call it "traffic." Back in the day, when direct-response marketing first evolved, marketers focused on lists. You figured out who your target customers were, and then you rented direct-mail lists of people who met those demographics and other criteria. This straightforward method worked for over a hundred years, and it still works today to some extent.

If I wanted to sell my new information product to financial planners, I would rent a physical mailing list of financial planners who bought something related in the last 30 to 60 days. Then I would write a sales letter, send it out to those people, and hope for the best. I might add a little more sophistication, but basically that's how we got "traffic" before the Internet.

The same thing happened with other media sources. I could network and go to tradeshows that had my dream customers there, and I would try to get those people to purchase my products. You could buy ads on tv or radio and target stations that your dream customers listened to. Or you could also target people in local areas with newspapers.

When the Internet came around, the whole dynamic changed. Not right away—it took a while for people to figure out how to use this new type of media to target people, convert them into leads and prospects, and then sell them products and services.

It started with Search Engines like yahoo and google. People would type in keywords to search for something they wanted to buy, and marketers like us could use those keywords to show our ads and get people into our funnels and grow their email lists.

As people's lists started to grow, then it became possible, similar to direct mail, where you could pay people to send out emails to their lists and push people into your funnels. The first 10 years of my career were focused on search engines and email lists.

Then, a new type of media came out that we called "social media." Inside of these social media platforms, we started shifting our focus from keywords to interest-based focus. Instead of focusing on search terms and guessing intent, now we can target people's interests directly on Facebook, Twitter, Instagram, and other platforms.

If I have a wrestling product, I can target people interested in wrestling. If I have a fishing product, I can target people interested in fishing. It only takes a couple of minutes to find huge lists of people who have already demonstrated their interests through Facebook groups, hashtags on Twitter and Instagram, or memberships in niche forums, then create ads to place in front of those people and drive them into your funnels.

That's how traffic has evolved the last decade or so since I've been online.

Secret #1: Your Funnel - How To Nail It, So You Can Scale It...

Before we get into traffic, it's essential to understand that no matter how much traffic you get, if you don't have a funnel that converts, all of the traffic in the world will ***NEVER*** help.

Most people that I've worked with directly start out by building super complex funnels. The first thing I want to warn you of is that the more complex your funnel is, the harder it is to make the tests and tweaks necessary to get it to convert right so you can scale it.

I want to stress that, initially, most of my funnels are very simple. Here's an example of a basic Tripwire funnel:

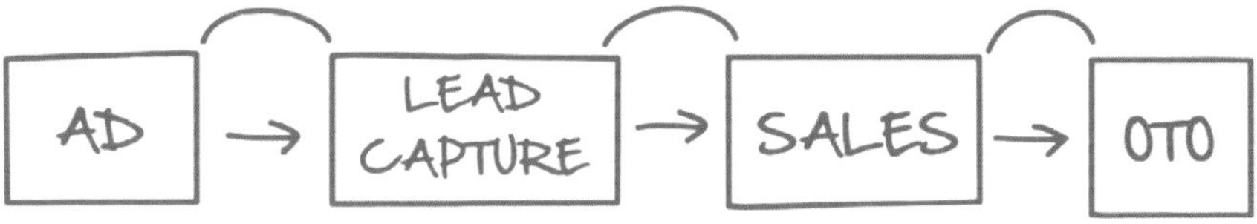

There's an ad, a landing page, a sales page, and then an upsell. One ad and three pages. Nothing more.

I like to keep it simple and easy so that after I pay for an ad, I can step back and see what worked and what didn't work. This is the KEY to being able to scale your traffic. Traffic is easy to get, getting it to convert is the part that most people struggle with.

So let's say I get 1,000 clicks on my ad. The next thing I need to know is how much I spent per click. You'll know this from Facebook or Google or wherever you buy your ads from. In this example, I spent $0.92 per click. So my total cost was $920.

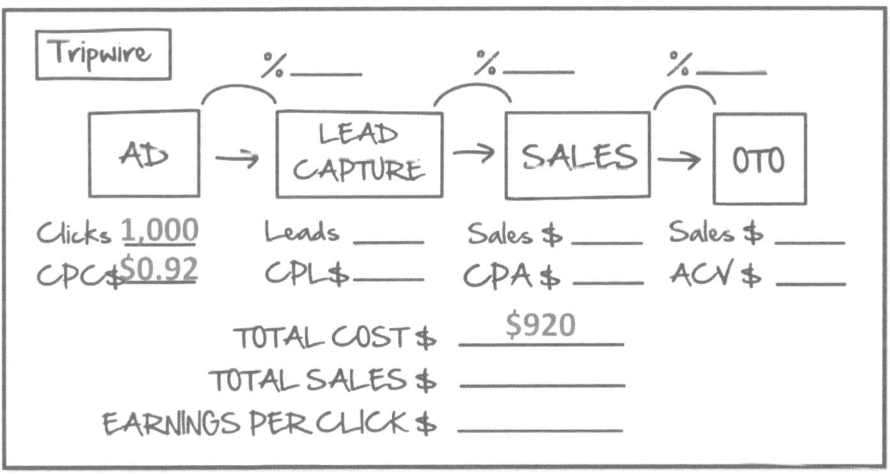

The next number I'm looking for is when people land on my lead capture page, how many people actually opted-in. Say I got 38% of the people to opt-in. That means I got 380 leads and my cost per lead (CPL) is $2.42.

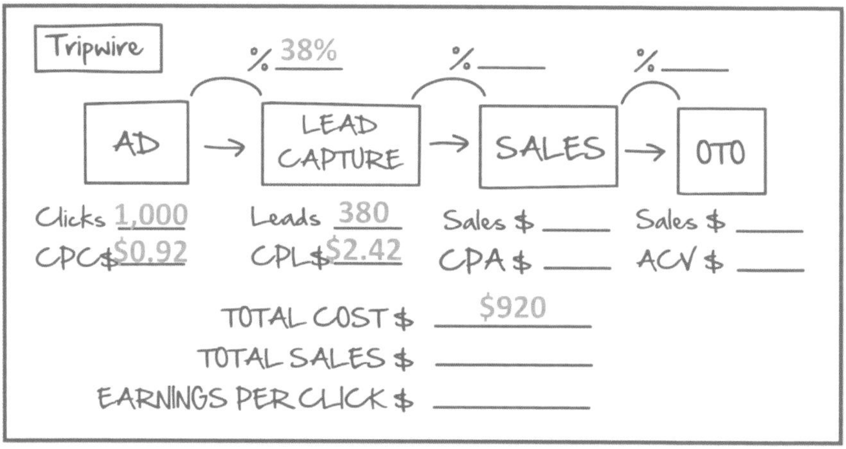

The next stat I want to know is how many people actually bought my product. In this example, let's say I got 9% of the leads to buy. That means I made 34 sales at $37. My cost per acquisition (CPA) was $27.

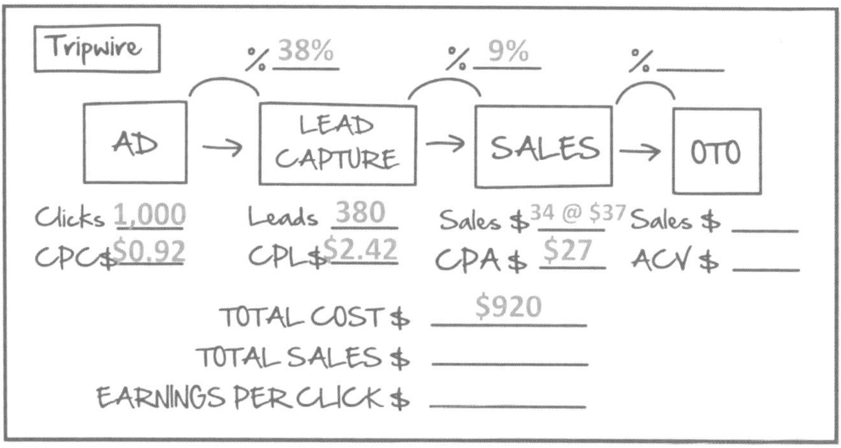

Then if I get 7% of people to take my upsell it means I got 3 people to buy at $197. This means my total sales come to $1,849. My average cart value (ACV) or the amount of money I made on average from each person who purchased my tripwire was $54. My earnings per click (EPC) was $1.85. Compare that to my Cost Per Click (CPC) of $0.92. This is an example of a winning campaign. I spent $0.92 and made back $1.85.

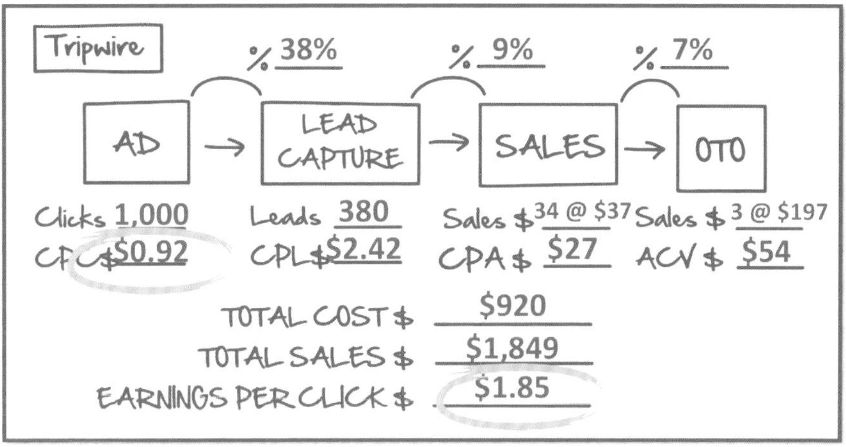

If I was driving traffic and those were my numbers, I'd say "OK, this campaign works." I would just keep driving more traffic to it until it stopped working.

Now here's the big secret to understand about getting your funnels to work, if it's not working at first, all is not lost. Usually there is one or two things that are clogging up the funnel. After you identify what those things are, then you can simply make the changes to the parts that are clogged, and then run another test. I normally have to repeat this three or four times until the funnel works, and then I can scale my campaigns.

For example, let's say I did the exact same funnel but instead of getting a 38% opt-in, I only get 11% of people to opt-in:

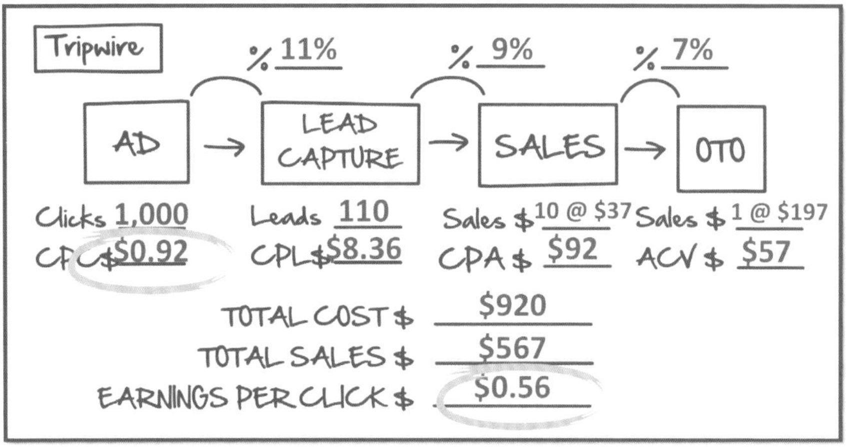

Notice how this campaign instantly becomes a loser? Even though everything else stayed the same, the low conversion on the landing page caused the whole funnel to not work. We only get 110 leads instead of 380. Our Cost Per Lead is now $8.36 instead of $2.42. This causes all the other costs to go up.

Now I'm spending $0.92 per click and I'm only making back $0.56. This is when people say "This funnel's broken! ClickFunnels is a scam! Russell doesn't know what he's talking about."

Or you can step back and look at this and ask which piece is broken. My cost per click was right. My conversions on my sales page and upsell was right. But the lead capture page was wrong. What can I do to tweak that to get it from 11% to 30% and beyond?

Once I fix that one piece, the rest of the funnel "magically" starts working.

The same thing is true if there's a mistake on your ad:

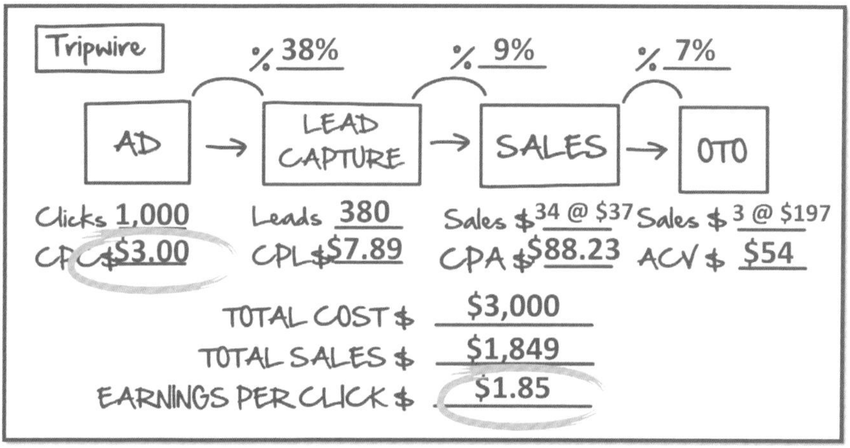

In this case, we spent $3.00 per click instead of $0.92. All the other metrics stayed the same so we still only made back $1.85 per click. This means the ad is broken. Maybe I spent too much on the ad? Maybe the ad wasn't engaging enough? But I can quickly identify what's broken.

Typically, I find that the entire funnel isn't broken, it's just one of these steps that's broken. So I go back and figure out what I can change to unclog the funnel. Once I make the right change, that's when all the traffic and sales start coming in.

Here's an example of an actual funnel that we created:

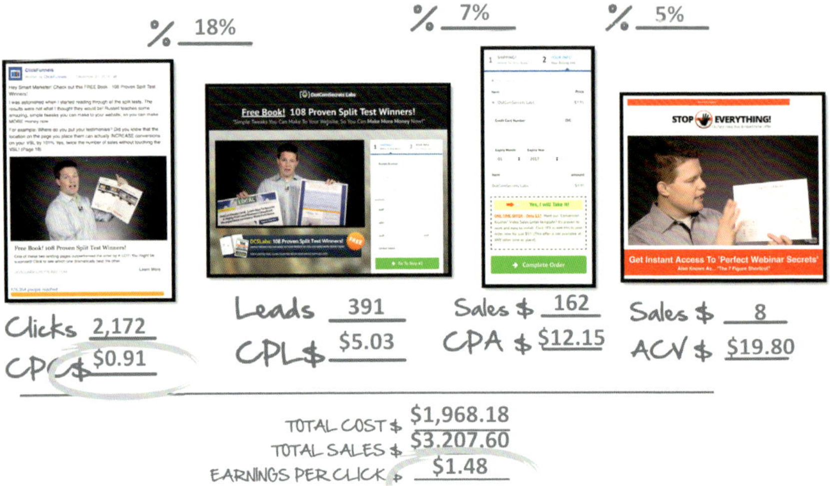

These numbers change based on ad source and a lot of other things but this will give you a picture of what a successful ad and funnel an look like.

So on this ad we got 2,172 clicks and we spent $0.91 per click. That means our total cost was $1,968.18. On the landing page we got 18% of the people to give us their contact information, which meant 391 leads. My cost per lead was $5.03.

7% of the leads actually purchased the book, which resulted in 162 sales. This means our cost per acquisition was $12.15.

5% of the people took the upsell resulting in 8 sales and an average cart value of $19.80.

So we made $3,207.60. My Earnings Per Click was $1.48 and my Cost Per Click was $0.91. Because of that, we've sold tens of thousands of copies of this book. We were able to drive a lot of traffic to it because we're making money on every click.

These funnel metrics are what gives you the ability to scale your traffic. If you don't understand this piece, it's almost impossible to get traffic.

Now we're going to switch gears and talk about the Dream 100 concept. This is what enables you to get unlimited people into your funnels.

Secret #2: The Dream 100

I wrote about the Dream 100 extensively inside the Expert Secrets book. I want to include that chapter here as well so you can understand how the process works. This is the key to getting almost unlimited traffic to each and every one of your funnels.

The million-dollar question everyone asks after they learn about funnels is "How do you actually get people into those funnels?" I had the same question when I got started. In fact, I remember asking a friend who was having a lot of success online at the time, "How do you create traffic?"

He smiled and said, "Russell, you don't need to create traffic, it's already there. People are already online. You just have to figure out how to get those people to leave where they are and come to you instead."

The wheels in my head started spinning. I started thinking about WHERE my dream customers were already congregating. I realized that, in most cases, the people I wanted to serve were already in the market looking for something. And if I could present them with MY new opportunity, I could get them to leave where they were and start following me.

About that same time, I heard about a concept called the "Dream 100" from one of my friends and mentors, Chet Holmes. Early in Chet's career, he worked for Charlie Munger, who you may know was Warren Buffet's partner in Berkshire-Hathaway. Chet sold advertising for one of the company's legal magazines. At the time, they were really struggling. Chet was working with a database of over 2,000 advertisers. He made calls and sent out materials every day. But they were still #16 out of 16 magazines in their industry. Dead last.

Then Chet got smart. He did some research and discovered that out of those 2,000 advertisers, 167 of them were spending 90% of their advertising budgets with his competitors. So he defined those 167 as his best buyers—the ones spending all the money in the industry. Once he figured that out, he stopped marketing to everybody and instead focused his time and efforts on those 167. He sent out direct-mail pieces with lumpy objects in them every two weeks, then he followed up with a few phone calls. Twice a month he'd mail, twice a month he'd call.

Now Chet was known for what he called "PHD"—Pig-Headed Determination. So he just kept going after those same people month after month. Because these were the biggest buyers, they were the hardest people to reach. But he didn't give up. After four months of following this strategy, he got zero response. (Pretty discouraging, right?)

Then in his fourth month, something changed. He landed his

first big account—Xerox. It was the biggest advertising buy ever for the company. By the sixth month, he had landed 29 of the 167. And with those 29, Chet doubled the sales over the previous year. They went from #16 to #1 in the industry in just over a year. And he kept doubling sales for the next three years.

Later on in his career, Chet wrote a screenplay and wanted to sell it to a big Hollywood studio. So he followed the same Dream 100 strategy. He researched and found 100 Hollywood producers, actors, directors, and other people who could make his film a reality. He focused on his Dream 100 list and relentlessly pursued these guys. And yes, eventually he did sell his film to one of those big studios.

So what does this have to do with you?

Well, when I first heard Chet explain how the Dream 100 worked, I realized that there were probably 100 people who already had MY dream customers. They had the traffic. I didn't need to create it, I just needed to figure out how to get those people to come and see my new opportunity instead.

The first step in this Dream 100 process was going back to Secret #1 in the Expert Secrets book. Remember when I created my new niche? We started with the three hot markets (health, wealth, and relationships).

From there, I drilled down into a sub-niche inside of one of those markets. Then within that sub-niche, I created my new opportunity.

I found that the key to the Dream 100 was to step back from my niche and go back up to the submarket level. Inside of that submarket are all the niches where my traffic is already congregating. All I needed to do was figure out WHO was controlling that traffic.

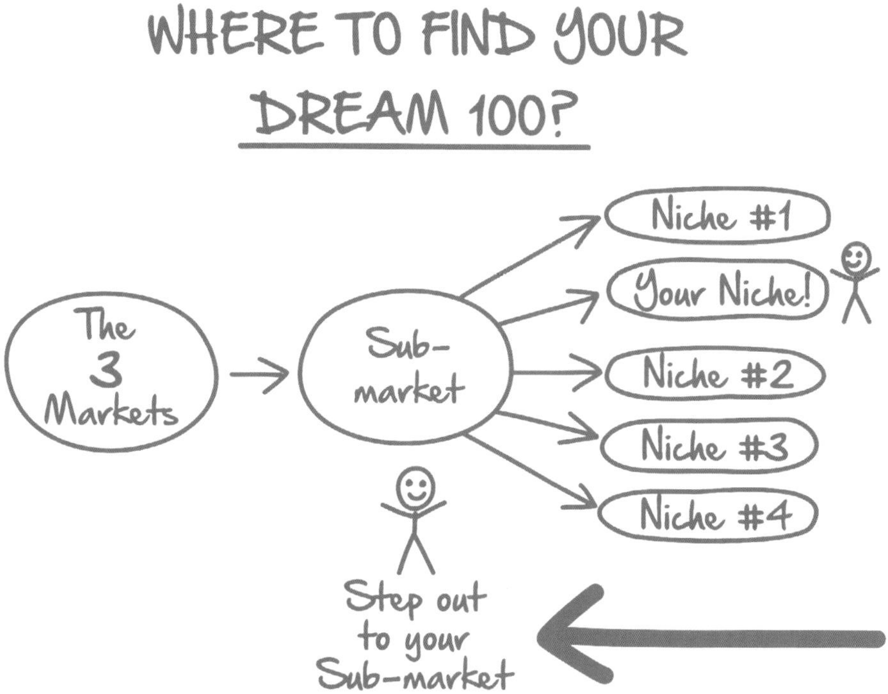

I quickly realized that the people who controlled that traffic were typically one of four types: list owners, bloggers, podcasters, or social media influencers (including YouTube, Instagram, Twitter, Facebook, etc.) I started searching and found list owners with email lists of 20,000 to 200,000 or more of my dream customers! Bloggers and podcasters who had millions of readers and listeners and social media influencers who could drive tens of thousands of clicks to anything they wanted to talk about. I saw their power, so I started to build out my Dream 100 list of these people and companies. Initially, I tried to find 25 list owners in my submarket, 25 bloggers, 25 podcasters, and 25 social media influencers.

After I filled out that list, I had the 100 people who already had the attention of those I wanted to serve. Then I put together a plan to infiltrate my Dream 100.

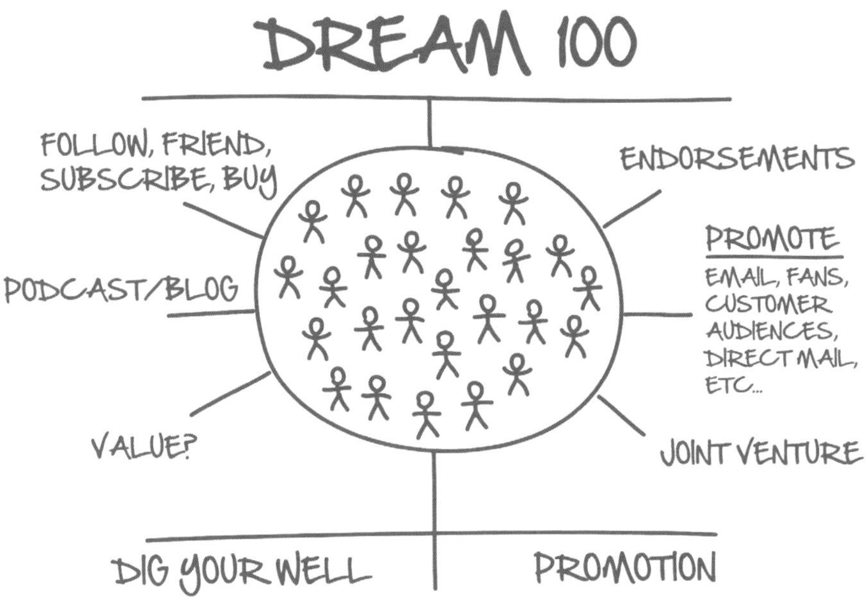

The first goal was to start building relationships with my Dream 100. As Harvey Mackay said, you want to "dig your well before you're thirsty". The WORST time to contact your Dream 100 is the day you need them to promote something for you. The best time to start building relationships is NOW. So when you are ready to ask them to promote you, that relationship will already be there.

Dig Your Well Strategy #1:

I started by following them, sending friend requests, subscribing to their emails lists, blogs, and podcasts, and buying their products. I wanted to put them on my radar so I could see what they were doing and get to know who they were before I made my first contact.

There is nothing worse than getting a meeting with an influencer and not knowing who they are, what they're working on, or what's important to them. I've met a lot of people through the years who somehow make it through my gatekeepers, but when they get on the phone, they're so focused on selling me something that we never get past the first few minutes. If you want to build a relationship with your Dream 100, you need to be prepared.

Dig Your Well Strategy #2:

After I know who they are and understand what's important to them, I want to give them a platform that helps to promote them, but at the same time gives me the ability to build a relationship with them. My favorite way to do that is to interview them for my podcast or my blog. I can usually get 30–60 minutes to ask them questions and build a relationship during that interview.

When I promote that interview, it helps them as well. Most of my best partners started with me interviewing them and then taking that relationship from the interview into Strategy #3.

Dig Your Well Strategy #3:

Now that I have a basic relationship with them, one of the main things I like to ask (and I learned this from Sean Stephenson) is what project they're working on that is most important to them at the moment. After they tell me, I figure out what extra value I can offer to help them reach their goal. And that's it. It's simple, but it's how great business relationships are built. I'm digging my well ***BEFORE*** I'm thirsty.

When should you start "digging your well"? Well, there is an old Chinese proverb that says, "The best time to plant a tree was 20 years ago. The second best time is now." You need to start this strategy NOW, no matter where you are in your business today.

After you've spent time digging your well, start looking for ways to leverage these relationships to gain access to their followers. If you have created a truly new opportunity that will serve their audience, then there are lots of ways you can work together. If you've "picked" a niche, then you'll likely be in direct competition with many of your Dream 100. But if you've created your niche—your new opportunity—then you should be complementary to most of them. This makes the promotion process a lot easier.

Promotion Strategy #1:

The easiest and best way to work with your Dream 100 is to get them to promote you and your new opportunity to their following. That's my #1 goal. I focus hard on the relationship. And when the time is right, I ask them to promote my webinar. I reach out to my Dream 100 by sending them a physical newsletter and package in the mail every month with information about the special promotions we are running and how they can be part of them. Even though my Dream 100 has grown to nearly 600 people, I still send a package and give them a call every month.

Not everyone on my Dream 100 will promote my products. In fact, many of them I can never even get on the phone. But I consistently market to them, because one YES can put me in front of their audience of hundreds of thousands of people or more! I've had times when one person on my Dream 100 has said yes, and within three months that relationship netted over a million dollars. It's worth consistently building relationships with those people. I would say that about 30% of the traffic into my funnels comes from this strategy.

Promotion Strategy #2:

While my main goal is to get my Dream 100 to promote my product, oftentimes they can't or won't, and that's okay. Over the past few years, most of the social networks have opened up their advertising platforms so I can promote to the fans and followers of specific people or companies. For example, I can go to Facebook and show ads to all the Tony Robbins fans (one of my Dream 100). You could go to Twitter and target Ashton Kutcher's followers (if he's in your Dream 100).

So I create specific ads to target the followers of each person on my Dream 100 list. Each network is different and they change frequently, so you'll need to stay on top of the networks you want to use. But if you go to www.FillYourFunnel.com, you can see the most up-to-date training for each network. About 40% of my traffic comes from this strategy.

Promotion Strategy #3:

So where does the last 30% come from? About 10% comes from marketing, search engine optimization, and other things we're doing each day, but the last 20% comes from something I learned called "integration marketing" from my first mentor, Mark Joyner. He wrote an awesome book by the same name that shows you how to integrate into the sales flow of your Dream 100.

If you look at the sales path that customers of people on your Dream 100 are going through, you can find places where it would make sense for your products or services to be offered. The idea is to integrate your offers into their natural sales funnel. Can you put one of your products on one of their thank-you pages? Can you put your ad in a PS on their emails? Could you co-create a product that you both promote and both get customers from? How can you integrate into your Dream 100 sales funnels? This way, it's not just one and done, instead you will get a continuous stream of customers. There are thousands of creative ways to integrate with your Dream 100.

There are so many ways to drive traffic and fill your funnels. But ALL my strategies are built on the foundation of the Dream 100. When you understand the strategy behind how and why this works, you can quickly and easily start getting customers into your funnel. Again, the tactics will change. But if you master the Dream 100 strategy, you will always be able to fill your funnels with new people.

Secret #3: Taking The Show On The Road

The last step after someone starts to get traffic, is they want ***MORE*** traffic. The biggest problem I see when people want to start to scale their campaigns, is they will get really excited about a particular platform when they first learn traffic. For example, they'll get excited about Facebook and so they'll start buying ads on Facebook and see some initial success. Often times they end up making a really good money on that platform. But there's a problem...

I've been doing this for over a decade and I've seen platforms come and go. I've had friends making five hundred thousand dollars a month or more from Google before the first "Google Slap," who then lost their businesses overnight. Most of them were not able to recover and are no longer in business anymore. I've had multiple friends who were making hundreds of thousands of dollars a month in SEO and then Google changed their algorithm and they got slapped and their business dried up over night.

I've seen the same thing happen in Facebook and platform after platform. If you put all your eggs in one platform, it gets really scary. I promise you Mark Zuckerberg is a good Dream 100 partner but he's just one of your Dream 100. If he decides he doesn't like you or your business, your income can dry up overnight. If there's not people consistently coming into your funnel then you're in trouble.

The first thing I want you to think about is having traffic from multiple sources. You need to reach a lot of people on different platforms.

I have a friend named Mary Ellen Tribby who is famous in my world for taking companies and scaling them quickly. A couple years back she worked at a company called Weiss Research and took them from $11 million a year in sales to $67 million in just 12 short months! She's done this process multiple times with multiple companies. The first time I got a chance to sit down and talk to her, the first thing I asked her was "how did you scale these companies so fast?"

She had an interesting answer. She said, "Russell, internet marketers like you are so smart on the one hand yet so dumb on the other hand."

"When you guys create a funnel it's the equivalent of writing a broadway play," she continued. You'll hire the best script writers, the most talented actors, you'll practice every single day for months, and then when it's finally ready to go live you'll promote it. You'll have a huge sold out audience on opening night. You give the show of a lifetime. The curtains drop and you get a standing ovation. Everyone leaves happy thinking it was one of the most amazing experiences of their life. Then the next morning you wake up and start writing your next play."

Then she told me, "All I do is take this funnel...this 'play' that you guys have created and I take that show on the road. I take it to Chicago, then New York and LA."

"That makes sense, but how do you do that with a funnel?" I asked.

As we continued talking I realized it has to do with this Dream 100 concept. It's targeting different people on different platforms. It's about getting new eyeballs to see your marketing and pushing them into your funnel over and over again.

In the Expert Secrets book I talked a lot about the model where we're doing the same webinar every single week.

When we have a funnel that's live, every single week our goal is to fill those funnels with new people. After they come into the funnel, we have other things on the backend that we'll sell them. But the #1 thing we're trying to do is to consistently fill our funnels with people from different platforms.

It all comes back to the Dream 100 strategy and focusing on building your audience in as many different places as possible. Start with a platform you like best and master it. If you like Facebook, then master that. Then move to YouTube and different platforms. The key is to consistently add to your traffic sources.

And that is how you fill your funnel. That is the strategy we've used to build companies that make millions of dollars per month. Now that you understand the strategy, you're roll as an entrepreneurs is to learn and master each of the tactics behind each source.

If you would like more information on how each platform works and the best way to those people into your funnels, then I want to invite you to join my free webclass called, "Fill Your Funnel."

Now that you understand the strategy, on this webclass you'll learn the tactics that make each of these platforms work for your company. You can register for this class free at: ***www.FillYourFunnel.com***

Thanks again for reading! I can't wait to hear your success story.

Russell Brunson